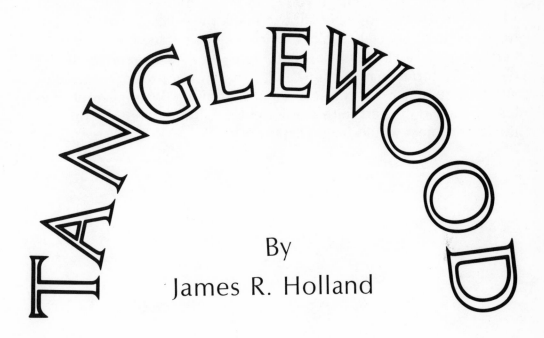

TANGLEWOOD

By

James R. Holland

Foreword by
Michael Tilson Thomas

Barre Publishers, Barre, Massachusetts 1973

The creation of this book involved the cooperation of many, many people. The author would like to thank the following individuals for their help. Special thanks to Mrs. Olga Koussevitzky, Thomas Perry, Jr., Mary H. Smith, Steve Solomon, Tom Waldman, Polly Pierce, Lee Broman and John Cahill. A note of appreciation should also be extended to the musicians and staff of the Boston Symphony Orchestra and the Berkshire Music Center, without whose cooperation this project would have been impossible.

Books by James R. Holland

The Amazon
Mr. Pops
Tanglewood

Copyright 1973 by James R. Holland
All rights reserved
Library of Congress Catalog Number 72-92470
International Standard Book Number 0-8271-7253-2
Design by Patricia Maka
Cover by Frank Stewart
Printed in the United States of America

This book is lovingly dedicated to Helen Holland.

Some typical Berkshire road signs located near the Massachusetts Turnpike in West Stockbridge.

At Tanglewood

The audience sees an elegant and impressive Festival of the Arts still tinged with the casual glamour of the 30s and 40s. The white suits and shoes of those who founded it and the striped Bermudas and thongs of those who now attend it pass in review around Saarinen's reverberant pie-slice in a ceremony of music, sun, and country. These are days of receptions, and late night suppers, and drinks in the tent, picnics on the lawn, players changing into their whites like members of an exclusive yachting society, and concerts: at least four a weekend, presented by the Boston Symphony Orchestra, colophons flying, and bells ringing, summoning the faithful from all over the grounds to. . . .

And then it is Sunday late and only green and quiet remain.

Then with the first of Monday, the Tanglewood that we who have studied there know so well returns. The crowds are gone but the tempo of activity, if anything, accelerates. Classes! Rehearsals! Umpteen zillion of them. The students swagger-stagger from one to another, complaining just a little too melodramatically about the difficulty of their schedule, and carry on the endless *symposium musicum* and *extra curricularium* (with rather more emphasis on the latter as the summer goes on).

You work in daily frenzy with living legends all around you — Aaron Copland, Leonard Bernstein, Seiji Ozawa, Gunther Schuller, Joseph Silverstein, Eugene Lehner, and practically everyone else you've ever heard of — all of them actually working with you, popping into rehearsals, reading pieces, talking about interpretation, or just rapping over a cold drink.

The pace is so swift you don't really know all that you've learned until it's over. You go home exhausted with a host of memories and new friends — and lessons learned — to find that back in your own pond you're a very different musician, and a different person.

For the original legends — the legend of Koussevitzky, of his devotion, idealism and faith in new and old music and musicians — have gotten to you. Somehow in the weeks on that greensward you have passed through his hands and your future directions, whether toward a new job, a new teacher, or a new will to work and to make music, will always bear that imprint.

Michael Tilson Thomas

The Berkshire Mountains of southwestern Massachusetts were once the home of the peaceful Mahican Indians. The Indians' original name, "Muhhekaneews," "the people of the great waters, continually in motion," was acquired during the time the tribe inhabited the Hudson River Valley. Their relatives were the same Indians described by Henry Hudson during his epic voyage up the river which bears his name.

Conflict with the warlike tribes of the Iroquois resulted in the Mahicans having to desert their Hudson River homeland and settle in the Berkshires, where they hunted in the unspoiled hills and fished in the crystal clear lakes.

In 1734, the Reverend John Sergeant chose his location wisely when he formed a mission called "Stockbridge," for of all the American Indians, the Mahicans were among the most readily converted to Christianity. By 1750, the Indian population at Stockbridge had risen from fifty to approximately 250 and included Wappingers, Mattabeseis, and Wyantonocs as well as the original Mahicans. From the time Stockbridge was incorporated as a town in 1739, these various Indian groups were referred to as "the Stockbridge Indians." They remained in the immediate area until about 1785, but had almost entirely disappeared by 1790 — moving first to New York State and finally settling in Wisconsin where nearly 1200 of their descendants can still be found.

The Mahicans fought as "Minutemen" during the American Revolution. Armed with their hatchets these Indians actually served in and around Boston and were the only tribe of Indians to stand on the side of the Americans during this crucial war. According to historian Charles Taylor, "a full company of Indians went to White Plains, under Captain Daniel Nenham, where four were slain and some died of sickness." Later the Mahicans became the first Indians to be granted United States citizenship.

The Mahicans are generally believed to be the "Mohegans" described by James Fenimore Cooper in his frontier novels. "Mohegan" was a common corruption of their proper name, "Muh-he-ka-neew."

After the Indians had gone, the area which is now the town of Lenox underwent a long period of slow growth — with farming as the main industry. Then, in 1803, the "Lenox Academy" was founded. This boarding school for boys was destined to play an important part in early life in Lenox, and established the area as an important educational center for nineteenth century America. Graduates of the school included the vice president of the Confederacy, the last president of the Republic of Texas, and many notable figures in law and education.

Around the middle of the nineteenth century began what many people refer to as the "heyday of Lenox" — the period when Lenox transformed itself from a sleepy farming community to "the Inland Newport." Samuel Gray Ward, a Boston banker, was the first outsider to build a summer residence in the area as an escape from the sweltering city. William A. Tappan, another Boston banker, soon followed his friend Samuel Ward and built a modest summer home on the edge of the Stockbridge Bowl. Tappan's property included a red cottage on the hill overlooking Lake Mahkeenac. In May of 1850, the Nathaniel Hawthorne family moved into this smaller house.

Hawthorne had recently published *The Scarlet Letter* and its introduction material had scandalized many of the citizens in his home town, Salem, Massachusetts. To escape the open hostility of his former neighbors, Hawthorne moved to the Berkshires. Nathaniel was rumored to be both moody and eccentric, and uninvited guests dropping in to meet the famous writer often went away convinced of the rumors' validity.

Although Hawthorne would live on the Tappan Estate for less than two years, it was to be a productive and happy time for him. During that brief period he completed *The House of the Seven Gables, Twice-Told Tales, A Wonderbook,* and started work on other books including *The Blithdale Romance.* Hawthorne's third child, Rose, was born in the picturesque cottage.

Dr. Oliver Wendell Holmes, another Pittsfield native, was a frequent visitor to Hawthorne's cottage. During Hawthorne's stay there, several other giants of the American literary world had summer residences in the Berkshires. Henry Wadsworth Longfellow married a woman from nearby Pittsfield; and although he never built a home on the land given him in Lenox as a wedding gift, he was a frequent visitor and summer resident in Pittsfield.

Perhaps one of the most unlikely occurrences in American literary history took place during a thunderstorm in August of 1850. While out picnicking at Monument Mountain, Nathaniel Hawthorne and Oliver Wendell Holmes took cover from the rain in a small crevice with an unknown writer from Pittsfield — Herman Melville. Both Holmes and Evert Duyckinck later commented on the instant friendship that developed between the two men — Melville was in awe of Hawthorne, but despite Melville's obvious adulation, Hawthorne sensed a literary kinship with his new admirer. They became great friends and spent hours discussing Melville's current problems in the writing of his novel, *Moby Dick.* By the time the book was published, Hawthorne had already praised the young author in the "Literary World," and to show his feelings for his new friend, Melville dedicated his masterpiece to Nathaniel Hawthorne, "in admiration of his genius."

After the birth of his daughter, Rose, in May of 1851 almost exactly a year after his arrival in the Berkshires, Hawthorne became restless and anxious to move. His writings include many references to his growing impatience with the scene. One reference read, "This is a horrible, horrible, most horrible climate . . . I detest it! I detest it!! I detest it!!! I hate Berkshire with my whole soul, and I would joyfully see its mountains laid flat!" In a letter to his sister he grumbled, "This is certainly the most unconvenient and wretched little hovel that I ever put my head in." This was quite a change from an earlier time when, in a happier mood, Hawthorne had expressed his pleasure with the scene outside his window with the words, "I cannot write in the presence of such a view . . ."

Hawthorne and his family left the Berkshires in November of 1851 but his influence was to be felt in Lenox for some time to come — for he was later to immortalize the area with his *Tanglewood Tales.* Tanglewood also became the new name for the Tappan Estate.

During this period, most wealthy members of American society were in the process of trying to emulate the life style of the European aristocracy. Modest summer houses such as the Tappans' Tanglewood home were replaced by what can only be described as American palaces. Land values skyrocketed, with the building of marble residences needing as many as a hundred servants to wait upon the whims of their owners. The depression and two world

Book for Review

Barre Publishing Company

TANGLEWOOD $4.95

PUBLICATION DATE:

July 6, 1973

Please observe publication date and send two copies of any notice to:

BARRE PUBLISHING COMPANY
South Street
Barre, Massachusetts
01005

Excerpts of up to 500 words are authorized for review purposes.

wars brought that glittering palatial era to a crashing close, but many of the former estates are today maintained as private schools — echoes of a past chapter in United States history.

The area felt a faint revival of its literary history in the early 1900's when Edith Jones Wharton — "The Lady of Lenox," as Henry James dubbed her — spent a total of five and a half years in residence there. The wife of Boston banker Edward Wharton, "the Lady" wrote about what she knew best; two of her better known works deal with the Berkshire scene. But both *Ethan Frome* and *Summer* had the same effect on Lenox residents as Hawthorne's *Scarlet Letter* had previously had on the Salem town folk. And after her marriage broke up, Mrs. Wharton gladly left Lenox and moved to Europe where she could be near her many literary friends.

The musical roots of present day Tanglewood can be traced back to 1934, when Henry Hadley conducted three August concerts at the Dan Hanna Farm in Stockbridge, Massachusetts. The concerts, which were performed by sixty-five members of the New York Philharmonic Orchestra, attracted only 3000 people, but were promptly deemed a success by local residents who promoted the series and called them the "Berkshire Symphony Festival." Eager to see the concerts continue because of the widespread attention (and influx of tourists) the festival attracted, several residents financed a second series of three concerts for the following summer. The 1935 season also enjoyed modest success, but it was obvious that a change was necessary in order to insure the survival of the Music Festival.

Dr. Hadley resigned as conductor of the annual event and the Trustees of the "Berkshire Music Festival" under the leadership of Miss Gertrude Robinson Smith and Mrs. Owen Johnson, both of Stockbridge, began their search for a fully established Symphony Orchestra to present the 1936 concert series. Various orchestras were considered, but an early sign of interest by Boston Symphony manager George E. Judd gave the Boston orchestra the first opportunity to perform at the Festival.

It is fortuitous that Dr. Serge Koussevitzky at this point foresaw the wonderful potential of an outdoor, summer festival. Dr. Koussevitzky was fully cognizant of how successful the Norfolk (Connecticut) Music Festival had been since its 1899 inception. He was also aware of the three-decade tradition of the South Mountain Music Festival in nearby Pittsfield, Massachusetts. Similar outdoor series had long been immensely popular throughout Europe and the astonishing success of young Arthur Fiedler with his Boston Esplanade concerts made Dr. Koussevitzky's decision about whether or not to perform at the Berkshire Musical Festival an easy one to make.

The Boston Symphony performed three concerts in the Berkshires that summer — in a circus tent set up at "Holmwood," a former Vanderbilt estate, in Lenox. The presence of such well-known persons as Dr. Koussevitzky and the Boston Symphony Orchestra attracted more than 15,000 eager music fans. From that point forward, Serge Koussevitzky's organizational genius and vision were to transform the rather modest Berkshire Music Festival into the present eight-week summer symphony season.

In 1936, it was a close friend of Koussevitzky, Mrs. Gorham Brooks, who with her aunt, Miss Mary Aspinwall Tappan, presented the Boston Symphony Orchestra with an unexpected, but very welcome Christmas present — the Tappan family's Berkshire estate, Tanglewood. Thus, in the summer of 1937, an expanded program of six concerts were presented under a tent at Tanglewood. Performing in a tent did, however, present certain problems. On the evening of August 12th, 1937, a violent thunderstorm drowned out the sound of the orchestra and damaged many of the orchestra's instruments. With a little coaxing from the shrewd Dr. Koussevitzky, Miss Gertrude Robinson Smith, President of the Festival, boldly took the stage and announced that a fund drive to build a permanent music stage was, from that moment, underway. By storm's end, over thirty-thousand of the needed one hundred thousand dollars had been pledged. Koussevitzky got his friend, Eero Saarinen, to design a music shed and support buildings. The construction cost of his building complex was prohibitive. But a local Stockbridge architect, Joseph Franz, modified the original plans so that the present-day, more modest music shed could be constructed. The building was quickly completed and on August 4, 1938, the Fifth Berkshire Symphonic Festival took place in the new shed.

By this time Dr. Koussevitzky's fertile mind had already formed plans for what he deemed "not only a local festival, but a national and an international one." He had also developed both the concept and desire to establish what he described as "a creative musical center, where the greatest living composers will teach the art of composition . . . the greatest conductors [will teach] the mystery of conducting orchestras and choruses . . . [and] a free cooperation of such an elite will . . . result in a creation of new and great values in art . . . [and] in the education and training of a new generation of American artists." A similar desire had previously been expressed by Henry Lee Higginson, the founder of the Boston Symphony Orchestra. In a statement in 1881 describing his hopes for the orchestra he included the following: "One more thing should come from this scheme, namely, a good honest school for musicians." Now at long last, Major Higginson's dream was to come to realization, through the unflagging efforts of Serge Koussevitzky.

Koussevitzky had a knack for recognizing talent and drawing it to him, and in 1940 the Berkshire Music Center officially opened. This summer academy is designed to give advanced music students and fully accomplished young musicians an opportunity to perfect their technique by working with the best professional people in their respective fields. From its beginning, the Center attracted the finest talent to its teaching staff. Aaron Copland, Gregor Piatigorsky, Hugh Ross, Boris Goldovsky, Lukas Foss, Robert Shaw, Isaac Stern, Gunther Schuller, along with the various members of the Boston Symphony, are only a few of the outstanding artists to teach at the Berkshire Music Center. In many instances the students themselves returned to continue the tradition of personal instruction that is the hallmark of the "Tanglewood Experience." The list of well-known former Tanglewood students reads like a musical *Who's Who.* Leonard Bernstein was the first Tanglewood conducting fellow to emerge as a giant in the musical world. Among the others who spent at least one summer of concentrated study at Tanglewood are: Leontyne Price, Robert Shaw, Michael Tilson Thomas, Burt Bacharach, Lawrence Foster, Thomas Schippers, Phyllis Curtin, Lorin Maazel, Claudio Abbado, and Seiji Ozawa. Roughly 10 percent of the musicians in major American symphony orchestras are Tanglewood alumni. The Berkshire Music Center, combined with the experimental opera workshop taking place in Tanglewood's "West Barn," may well be the key to the continuing growth of Tanglewood into the great Music Center foreseen by its founders. As Nathaniel Hawthorne prophetically noted more than a hundred years ago, "Tanglewood will remain . . . but occupied by an entirely different family."

It was these trees — or others like them — which inspired Nathaniel Hawthorne to name the area "Tanglewood."

Berkshire Music Center students entertain themselves while waiting for a shuttle bus back to their dormitory.

14

The formal gardens provide younger Tanglewood visitors with an Alice-in-Wonderland opportunity to explore the manicured hedge-world. Slightly older guests pause to cool their feet in one of the garden's several pools.

A skilled member of the grounds crew lovingly looks after the 210 acres of greenery.

The Main House was built by wealthy Bostonian William Tappan in 1849 as a summer home. The building now provides a variety of offices and music rooms for the Berkshire Music Center.

18

The famous Tanglewood pines tower over the former estate's main gate.

Looking south toward Lake Mahkeenac.

Early arrivals for the evening concert.

20

There was a time when visitors arriving at Tanglewood without formal dress were issued paper neckties, or long paper skirts, as the gender demanded. Those days are gone, except for an occasional and pleasant reminder of times past.

There is no easily identifiable Tanglewood type. All manner of people come to Tanglewood for all kinds of reasons. Some visitors come strictly to listen to the music, others come just for a relaxing day enjoying the lush grounds and cool mountain breezes, and some young parents bring their children for an afternoon picnic and an introduction to symphony music.

As many as twenty thousand music lovers have attended a single symphony concert at Tanglewood. Many listen from inside the huge music shed, but most find spots on the lawn outside the fan-shaped music hall.

A sun tan is one of the by-products of an afternoon concert in the Berkshires. Another might be a new friendship. People-watching also rates high as a form of entertainment during intermission.

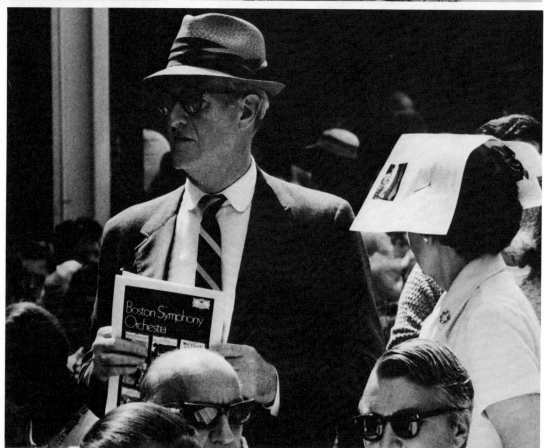

Outdoor dining is developing into quite an art for Tanglewood patrons. Multi-course meals, champagne, and soft candlelight dinners are not uncommon.

(Left) Jim Kiley is pleased with the efforts of his grounds crew.

Eugene Ormandy conducts the Boston Symphony Orchestra. He is a great favorite of the Tanglewood music audiences.

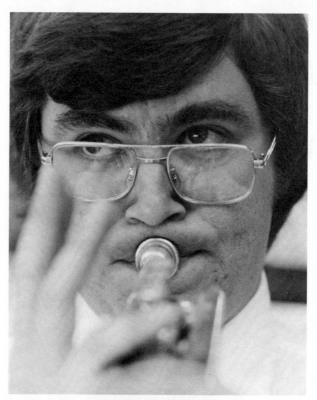

William Steinberg took over as Music Director of the Boston Symphony in 1969.
Three years later he completed his tenure with the BSO and marked the occasion
with a special Beethoven weekend at Tanglewood. The series proved to be one
of the most popular events in Tanglewood concert history.

Colin Davis, one of the principal guest conductors for the BSO, grins with delight as the audience resoundingly approves his performance. Orchestra personnel director Bill Moyer, Music Librarian Victor Alpert, and stage manager Al Robison look on.

Backstage between encores, Seiji Ozawa waits with guest soloist Deborah O'Brien before taking one final bow. In the background, Mrs. Ozawa is greeted by Mrs. Koussevitzky. Seconds later, Seiji notices his wife's arrival and welcomes her.

In a tent at the northeast corner of the music shed coffee and rolls are served to the members of the orchestra and the Tanglewood chorus during concert intermission.

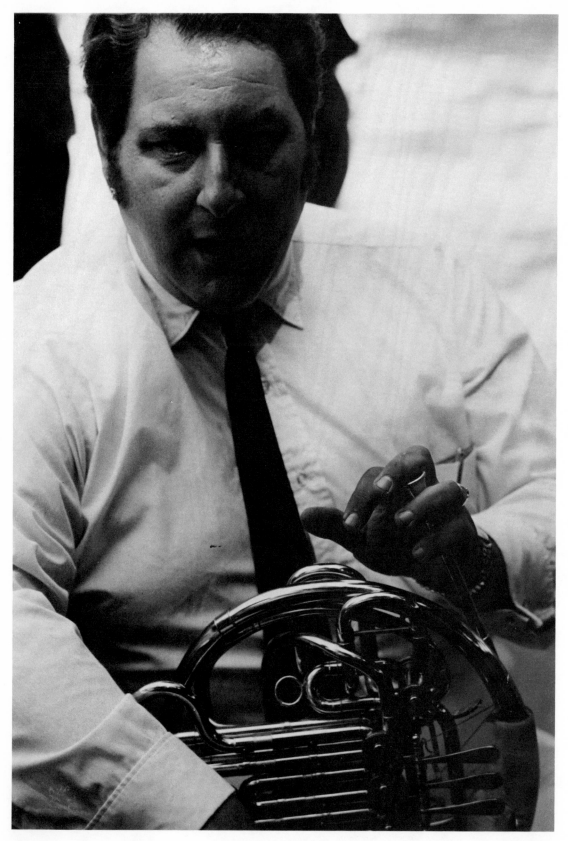

Prior to each concert and during breaks, most members of the Boston Symphony spend their time either practicing, chatting with friends or relatives, or in some cases, minding their grandchildren. With a group as talented as the individual members of the BSO, conversation usually covers an incredibly wide spectrum of topics. Members of the orchestra include Ph.D. physicists and chemists, lobster fishermen, gourmet cooks, ordained ministers, licensed pilots, and devotees of photography, woodcarving, and art collecting.

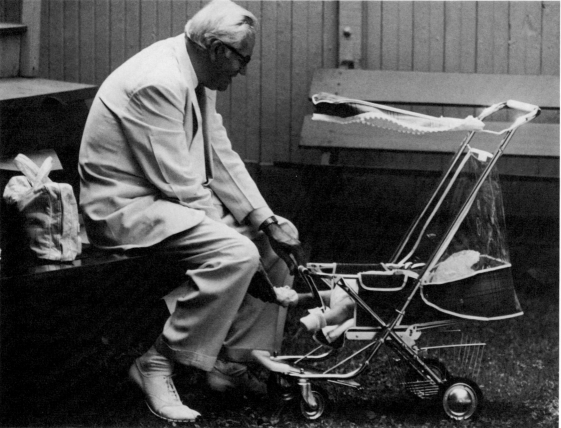

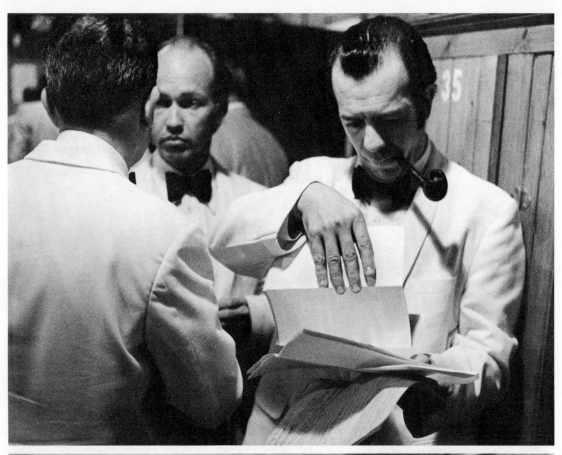

With Michael Tilson Thomas watching, concert master Joseph Silverstein and
first cellist Jules Eskin rehearse one of Aaron Copland's compositions for a
special concert prelude.

Mr. Copland and Michael Tilson Thomas discuss the rehearsal's progress during an orchestra break.

BSO violinist Leonard Moss.

Aaron Copland, Michael Thomas, and Phyllis Curtin in the green room preparing for Mr. Copland's "Twelve Poems of Emily Dickinson."

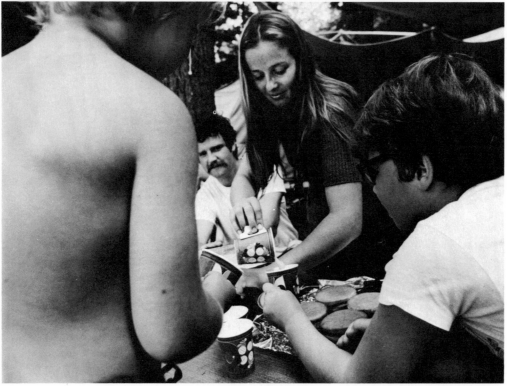

Most orchestra members rent nearby houses during the eight-week Tanglewood season, but house trailers, cabins, and tents are fast becoming equally popular summer addresses. Luis Leguia and family, following the advice of fellow musician John Barwicki (the first BSO member to camp out during the season), set up camp on the shores of Lake Mahkeenac.

53

Mr. James Weeks is only one of several professional artists who direct and assist the Boston University students with their studies.

Fisheye view of a young artist painting near the "East Barn." The former stable has been converted into several large studios for use by art students.

54

A striped carnival tent is located at the southeast corner of the music shed. The tent provides a resting place for "Friends" and special guests of Tanglewood. On some afternoons, members of the orchestra provide "Talks and Walks" for interested listeners. Here, Harry Ellis Dickson, First violinist and Assistant POPS conductor, reminisces about his adventures with the BSO.

Aldo Ceccato, a dedicated bicyclist, arrives at the Music Shed to conduct the BSO. Other popular modes of transportation include walking and motor scooters.

Daniel Gustin, administrator of the Berkshire Music Center, discusses the music school's policy with a visiting composer.

Seiji Ozawa conducts the Berkshire Center Orchestra comprised of gifted young musicians.

Maestro Ozawa relaxing after a concert. Within minutes of the concert's conclusion, Seiji has changed into his blue jeans, pull-over shirt, and tennis shoes.

One of the most interesting offices at Tanglewood is that of Thomas D. Perry, Jr., (right) manager of the Boston Symphony Orchestra. His office, which is actually a tiny wooden cabin, has walls covered with orchestra memorabilia.

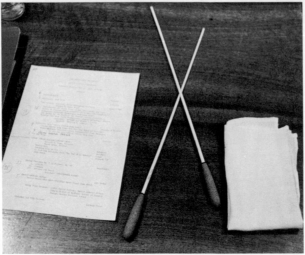

(Opposite) As do most of the guest conductors, Mr. Fiedler and his wife stay at the nearby Holiday Inn.

Arthur's long-time friend John Cahill usually joins the Fiedlers for their annual Tanglewood Pension Fund Concert.

One of the least known, but most interesting activities at Tanglewood is the Music Theater Project. Co-funded by the Martha Baird Rockefeller Fund and the National Opera Institute, the 1972 program included the world premiere of Robert Selig's "Chocorua." Based on events which took place in eighteenth century New England, the unusual opera was jointly commissioned by the Berkshire Music Center and the Fromm Music Foundation.

Here, the cast and director take their well deserved bows after the premiere performance. The opera's protagonist, the Indian, Chocorua, was played by Timothy Nolen whose great uncle was Red Cloud, chief of the Sioux nation, and victor at "the Little Big Horn."

(Above) Director Ian Strasfogel.

Prior to the audience's arrival, members of the opera cast can usually be found outside the renovated barn practicing their music. Here, William Neill warms up his voice for his portrayal of Nero in "The Coronation of Poppea."

Gunther Schuller chatting with a member of the opera's cast.

(Photo by Helen Devine.)

Like the nearby "East Barn," the "West Barn" has also been converted to a new use, but instead of art studios the "West Barn" houses a complete theater. Here, some of the brightest young talent in opera can perfect their technique in the production of their own shows.

Hawthorne Cottage is a picturesque two-story wooden house overlooking Lake Mahkeenac. The house is an exact replica of the one Nathaniel Hawthorne and his family occupied from summer 1850 to mid-winter 1851. The original structure was destroyed by fire in 1890, and rebuilt in 1943 by the American Federation of Music Clubs, Mrs. Guy Patterson Gannett, president. The house now serves as a studio and classroom building for the Berkshire Music Center.

Bruno Maderna meeting with a class of conducting fellows in Hawthorne Cottage.

Hawthorne Studio.

Aerial photograph showing Tanglewood in relation to Lake Mahkeenac. The BSO
maintains a private beach and campgrounds for its staff at the edge of the lake.

72

Looking south across the tiny Tanglewood beach from which Nathaniel Hawthorne and his four-year-old son Julian once launched model sailing ships.

(Photo by Helen Devine)

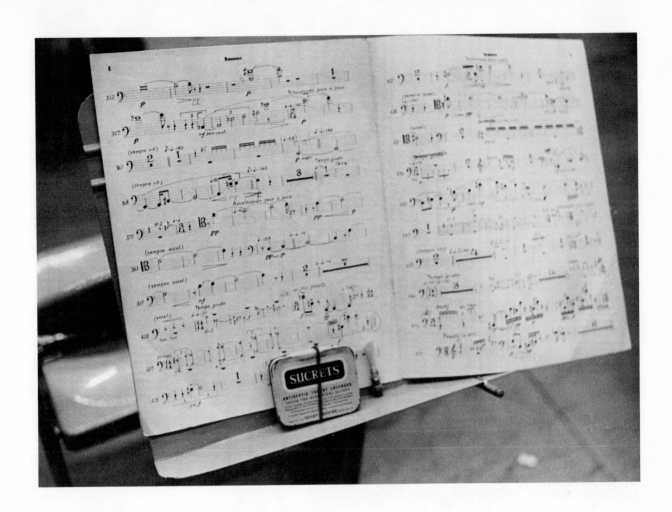

75

Gunther Schuller rehearses with a student orchestra for the Tanglewood debut of one of his compositions. Mr. Schuller, President of the New England Conservatory of Music, has proved an enormous help to the Berkshire Music Center. Through the years, he has served in a variety of capacities including both teacher and advisor to what has been called "the Tanglewood academy of music."

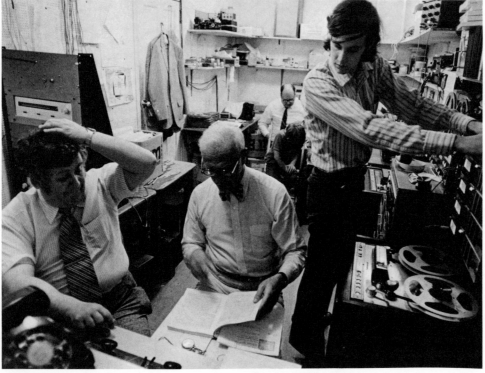

Inside the Tanglewood music shed is WCRB's recording and broadcasting studios.
Here the magic sound of the BSO emanates to millions of radio listeners.

78

William Pierce, the "Voice" of the Boston Symphony Orchestra.

Leonard Bernstein as seen from a seat in the orchestra during an open rehearsal. Conductor and composer Bernstein has been an important force as instructor, director, and advisor in post-Koussevitzky Tanglewood.

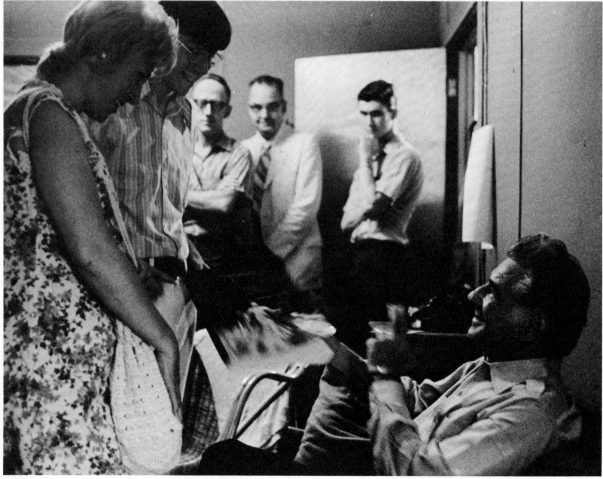

Symphony musicians seconds after the last bow.

Leonard Bernstein signs autographs in the conductor's room of the music shed.

Mrs. Leonard Bernstein listens to friends during an after-the-concert party held at the home of Mr. and Mrs. Todd Perry.

Maestro Bernstein emphasizing a point.

Mrs. Thomas Perry, Mrs. Koussevitzky, and friends.

86

The concert is over.

Concert goers patronizing the Tanglewood Music and Bookstore.

Students at the Berkshire Music Center.

The old Congregational Church in Lenox, where Serge Koussevitzky's grave site is marked by a giant maple tree.

Weddings at Tanglewood are uncommonly beautiful. The wedding of Julie Anderson to Steven Solomon, a member of the orchestra staff, took place in the grove of birch trees just east of the Main House, and guests included many musicians and staff members of the Boston Symphony Orchestra.

"Tanglewood is my blood and tears — and my greatest joy."

— *Serge Koussevitzky*

This book, not to mention Tanglewood, would not have been possible without the following members and staff of the Boston Symphony Orchestra:

First violins
Joseph Silverstein
concertmaster
Charles Munch chair
Jerome Rosen
Max Hobart
Rolland Tapley
Roger Shermont
Max Winder
Harry Dickson
Gottfried Wilfinger
Fredy Ostrovsky
Leo Panasevich
Sheldon Rotenberg
Stanley Benson
Alfred Schneider
Gerald Gelbloom
Raymond Sird
Ikuko Mizuno
Cecilia Arzewski

Second violins
Clarence Knudson
Fahnestock chair
William Marshall
Michel Sasson
Ronald Knudsen
Leonard Moss
William Waterhouse
Ayrton Pinto
Amnon Levy
Laszlo Nagy
Michael Vitale
Spencer Larrison
Marylou Speaker
Darlene Gray
Ronald Wilkison
Harvey Seigel

Violas
Burton Fine
Charles S. Dana chair
Reuben Green
Eugene Lehner
George Humphrey
Jerome Lipson
Robert Karol
Bernard Kadinoff
Vincent Mauricci
Earl Hedberg
Joseph Pietropaolo
Robert Barnes
Yizhak Schotten

Cellos
Jules Eskin
Philip R. Allen chair
Martin Hoherman
Mischa Nieland
Stephen Geber
Robert Ripley
Luis Leguia
Carol Procter
Jerome Patterson
Ronald Feldman
Joel Moerschel
Jonathan Miller

Basses
Henry Portnoi
William Rhein
Joseph Hearne
Bela Wurtzler
Leslie Martin
John Salkowski
John Barwicki
Robert Olson
Lawrence Wolfe

Flutes
Doriot Anthony Dwyer
Walter Piston chair
James Pappoutsakis
Paul Fried

Piccolo
Lois Schaefer

Oboes
Ralph Gomberg
John Holmes
Wayne Rapier

English horn
Laurence Thorstenberg

Clarinets
Harold Wright
Pasquale Cardillo
Peter Hadcock
E♭ clarinet

Bass clarinet
Felix Viscuglia

Bassoons
Sherman Walt
Ernst Panenka
Matthew Ruggiero

Contra bassoon
Richard Plaster

Horns
Charles Kavaloski
Charles Yancich
Harry Shapiro
David Ohanian
Ralph Pottle

Trumpets
Armando Ghitalla
Roger Voisin
André Come
Gerard Goguen

Trombones
William Gibson
Ronald Barron
Gordon Hallberg

Tuba
Chester Schmitz

Timpani
Everett Firth

Percussion
Charles Smith
Arthur Press
Assistant timpanist
Thomas Gauger
Frank Epstein

Harps
Bernard Zighera
Ann Hobson

Librarians
Victor Alpert
William Shisler

Stage Manager
Alfred Robison

Personnel Manager
William Moyer

Thomas D. Perry, Jr.
Manager

Thomas W. Morris
Assistant Manager,
Business Affairs

David Rockefeller, Jr.
Assistant Manager,
Audience & Public Affairs

Mary H. Smith
Assistant Manager,
Concerts & Artists

Forrester C. Smith
Development Manager

Daniel R. Gustin
Administrator of
Educational Affairs

Donald W. MacKenzie
Operations Manager,
Symphony Hall

James F. Kiley
Operations Manager,
Tanglewood

Richard C. White
Assistant to
the Manager